HELLO KITTY

My First Cookery Book

This book is all about cooking fun. Here are a few things that you need to remember!

Be careful!

1. Never run in the kitchen.
2. Never touch anything electrical with wet hands.
3. Never touch anything sharp or hot without a grown-up helper.
4. Always make sure your grown-up helper does any chopping.
5. Always ask your grown-up helper to place things in and out of the oven and wear oven gloves when handling anything hot.
6. Make sure you turn everything off once you have finished.

Before you start!

1. Wash your hands with soap in warm water and dry them on a clean towel before handling food. Always wash your hands after handling any raw meat or fish.
2. Make sure all work tops are clean and tidy. If you spill anything, wipe it up straight away!
3. Put on your apron, tie your hair back and roll up your sleeves.
4. Read the recipe you have chosen all the way through to make sure you understand what you have to do. Make sure you have all the ingredients.

Finally: always ask an adult before you start cooking!

Hello Kitty ××

First published in the UK by Harper Collins Children's Books in 2012

1 3 5 7 9 10 8 6 4 2

1976, 2012 SANRIO CO., LTD.

ISBN: 978-0-00-745150-0

HarperCollins *Children's Books*

BREAKFAST

LUNCH

DINNER

TREATS

Breakfast

In this section you'll find delicious recipes to get your day off to a yummy start!

Muesli

Makes enough for 4

You will need:

✓ 3 cups oats

✓ 1 cup mixed nuts

✓ 2 cups dried fruit

(If you don't have a cup you can use a coffee mug!)

What to do:

1. Tip the oats into a large airtight container.
2. Add the nuts and dried fruits and mix well.
3. To serve, give the container a gentle shake then spoon a portion into a bowl. Pour over milk or yoghurt and top with chopped fruit.

★ TOP TIP ★

Make sure your grown-up helper does any chopping!

MILK

2

Pancakes

Makes 8

You will need:

2 cups plain flour

2 cups milk

2 eggs (beaten)

Dash of oil for each pancake

Flour

M

What to do:

1. Place the flour in a bowl.
2. Break in the eggs.
3. Add the milk and mix together.
4. Get a grown-up helper to add a teaspoon of oil to a hot pan. Ask the grown-up helper to add 2 tablespoons of the mixture per pancake (or enough to cover the bottom of the pan), swirling it around until any gaps are filled.
5. When the pancake doesn't stick to the bottom any more, get your grown-up helper to turn it over (either with a spatula or flip it!).
6. Get your grown-up helper to leave it on the heat for approximately 30 seconds and then it's ready to eat! Repeat these steps for each pancake.
7. If you're not going to eat them straight away you can stack them with pieces of greaseproof paper in between.

Chocolate Croissants

Makes 12

You will need:

Chocolate (or chocolate spread)

1 pack of puff pastry

1-2 tbsp milk

What to do:

1. Ask your grown-up helper to pre-heat the oven to 200°C/Gas Mark 6.
2. Roll out your puff pastry until it's roughly the same thickness as a pound coin.
3. Ask your grown-up helper to cut the pastry into 6 squares, and then cut each square diagonally into a triangle.
4. Place a square of chocolate (or a teaspoon of chocolate spread) near the longest edge of the triangle.
5. Carefully roll the pastry up from the longest side towards the point of the triangle. Seal the point of the triangle to the rest of the pastry by pinching it gently.
6. Curl the ends so it looks like a croissant.
7. Brush the tops of the croissants with milk to make them extra golden.
8. Ask your grown-up helper to put them in the oven for 12-15 mins.

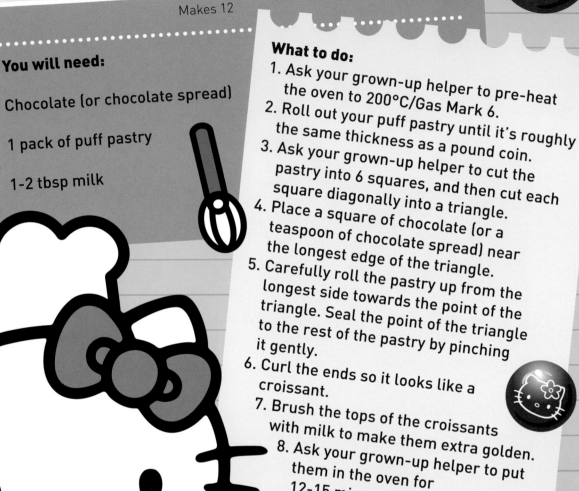

TOP TIP

MILK

Eat the croissants warm so the chocolate is melted. Mmmm!

4

Baked Dippy Eggs

Makes enough for 4

You will need:

1 large slice of ham

8 small spinach leaves

8 cherry tomatoes

4 eggs

1 matchbox-sized piece of Cheddar cheese

4 slices of bread, toasted, buttered and cut into dippers to eat with the dippy eggs

Butter

What to do:

1. Ask your grown-up helper to switch the oven on to 180°C/Gas Mark 4.
2. Put 4 ramekins in front of you. Tear the ham and spinach into strips and put some in each ramekin.
3. Squash the cherry tomatoes into a bowl using your fingers. (They may squirt so mind your clothes!) Divide the squashed tomatoes into each ramekin.
4. Break an egg into a bowl. Tip the egg carefully into one of the ramekins. Do the same with the other 3 eggs and the other ramekins.
5. Grate the cheese and sprinkle some on top of each egg.
6. Ask a grown-up helper to put the ramekins on a baking tray in the oven for 15-18 mins until the egg white has set.

Smoothie

Makes 1 smoothie

You will need:

Fruit (such as bananas, apricots strawberries, raspberries)

2 tbsp yoghurt

100 ml milk

TOP TIP

If you want your smoothie to be thicker – simply add less milk!

MILK

What to do:

Ask your grown-up helper to pop all the ingredients into a blender and blend.

Make a cute egg vase
Use eggshells to make a cute vase!

You will need:

An empty eggshell

Some paints and paintbrushes

Some small flowers

An egg cup

What to do:

1. Carefully rinse out the eggshell and leave it to dry.
2. Once the eggshell is dry, you can get creative! Use paints to decorate it however you like. You can use glue to stick on little shells or pieces of tissue paper.
3. Let the paint dry, before carefully pouring in some cold water, filling the egg to about halfway.
4. Pop in some little flowers and then place the eggshell into an egg cup to display it.

6

Lunch

Try these tasty recipes to make any lunch time scrumptious.

Potato Salad/ Pasta Salad

Makes enough for 4

You will need:

400g cold boiled potatoes (chopped) or cold cooked pasta

3 tbsp mayonnaise or sour cream

Tin of sweetcorn

1 pepper (chopped)

1 stick of celery (chopped)

2 spring onions (chopped)

4 mushrooms (optional)

A handful of peas

1 tsp wholegrain mustard

SWEET CORN

What to do:
1. Add the potatoes or pasta and the pepper, celery, onions, mushrooms, sweetcorn and peas to a bowl.
2. Add the mustard and the mayonnaise or sour cream and mix gently until all the potatoes or pasta are covered.

TOP TIP

To make it extra tasty, you could add tuna or bacon to this!

Open Sandwiches

Makes 4

You will need:

4 thick slices of ciabatta or crusty bread

Choice of toppings:
* ✖ Tuna and sweetcorn
* ✖ Tomato and mozzarella
* ✖ Ham and cheese

TOP TIP

What to do:

1. Take a thick slice of bread and carefully place your toppings on top. Remember not to pile them too high otherwise it's difficult to eat!

To make your open sandwiches really special, you could bake your very own bread! See p10!

Chicken Roll Ups

Makes 1

You will need:

1 wrap or tortilla

1-2 tbsp houmous

3 slices cooked chicken breast

¼ avocado taken out of its skin

3 cherry tomatoes

Cheddar cheese, grated to make about 1 tbsp

What to do:

1. Put a wrap on a plate. Spread the houmous onto the middle of it using a spoon.
2. Tear up the chicken (or ask a grown-up helper to do this) and put it in a line down the middle of the wrap.
3. Ask your grown-up helper to chop the avocado and put it next to the chicken.
4. Squish the tomatoes onto the wrap by squeezing them and tearing them in half. (They might squirt so mind your clothes!). Sprinkle on some cheese.
5. Roll up the wrap and press it down firmly. Ask your grown-up helper to cut it in half for you.

Soda Bread

Makes 1 loaf

You will need:
- ✓ 170g/6oz self-raising wholemeal flour
- ✓ 170g/6oz plain flour
- ✓ ½ tsp salt
- ✓ ½ tsp bicarbonate of soda
- ✓ 290ml/ ½ pint buttermilk

What to do:
1. Ask your grown-up helper to heat the oven to 200°C/Gas Mark 6.
2. Tip the flours, salt and bicarbonate of soda into a large bowl and stir.
3. Make a well in the centre and pour in the buttermilk, mixing quickly to form a soft dough.
4. Tip out on to a lightly floured surface and knead briefly.
5. Shape into a round shape and flatten the dough slightly before placing it on a lightly floured baking sheet.
6. Ask a grown-up helper to cut a cross on the top and place it in the oven for about 30 mins until golden or it sounds hollow when tapped.
7. Cool on a wire rack.

TOP TIP

When it's cool enough, ask your grown-up helper to cut you a slice and spread on some jam for a yummy snack!

Cheese Twists

Makes approx. 20

You will need:

1 pack of puff pasty

100g Cheddar cheese (grated)

What to do:

1. Get your grown-up helper to pre-heat the oven to 200°C/Gas Mark 6.
2. Roll out the puff pastry until it's about 1cm thick.
3. Sprinkle the grated cheese evenly over half the pastry.
4. Fold over the pastry, and roll it out like you did in step 2.
5. Get your grown-up helper to cut the pastry into strips.
6. Now use your hands to twist each strip.
7. Place on a baking tray.
8. Get your grown-up helper to place in the oven and bake for 10-12 mins.

Yummy!

TOP TIP

These yummy twists are delicious hot or cold.

LUNCH

Treasure Trail

Your friends will love this treasure hunt!

You will need:

Pencil

4 envelopes

4 small slips of paper

Yummy treasure

CLUE 1

CLUE 2

1. A treasure hunt needs clues. The first clue will lead the hunters to the second clue. The second leads the hunters to the third clue and so on, until the hunters find the treasure. Look around your house and decide on three places where you can hide a clue and one in which you can hide the treasure.

My hiding places are:

a. ....

b. ....

c. ....

d. Shh! This is where I've hidden the treasure! ....

....

2. Write out your clues and put them in envelopes – number them one to four.
3. Hide clues two, three and four in the places you've picked. Now, hide your treasure – make sure no one's looking!
4. Tell your friends or family that you have hidden some yummy treasure for them somewhere in the house and give them clue number one.
5. As your friends are searching, follow them. If they get stuck give them extra clues by saying 'hotter' when they are getting closer to the hiding place and 'colder' when they are further away!

Colder!

Hotter!

?

CLUE 3

★ TOP TIP ★

Once your yummy treats have been found, why not take them outside and have a nice picnic!

13

Dinner

These meals are really easy to make and taste amazing!

Sausage Meatballs

Makes enough for 4

You will need:
4 sausages or veggie sausages

What to do:

1. Get your grown-up helper to pre-heat the oven to 180°C/Gas Mark 4.
2. Lightly oil a baking tray.
3. Use your hands to squeeze the sausages out of their skins.
4. Now roll the sausage meat into small balls, about the size of a marble, shaping them tightly.
5. Place the balls carefully on the baking tray.
6. Ask your grown-up helper to put them in the oven for about 20 mins.

TOP TIP

Serve with pasta or salad. These are extra tasty with a tomato sauce. See p19.

Cheesy Mustard Chicken

Makes enough for 2

If you don't have any tomatoes on the vine, any tomatoes will do!

You will need:

100g Cheddar cheese (grated)

2 tbsp milk

2 tbsp wholegrain mustard

2 chicken breasts

6 tomatoes (still on the vine)

What to do:

1. Ask your grown-up helper to heat the oven to 180°C/Gas Mark 4.
2. Mix the cheese with the milk and mustard.
3. Smear the mixture on top of the chicken breasts.
4. Place in an oven dish together with the vine tomatoes (still on the vine so they hold together and look pretty).
5. Ask your grown-up helper to place in the oven for 20 mins.

Kiss the Chef

DINNER

15

Healthy Salad

Makes enough for 4

You will need:

600g tomatoes (chopped)

300g ciabatta (stale is best)

1 garlic clove (chopped) (optional)

Handful of olives

4 roasted red peppers (from a jar)

A few leaves of basil

100ml olive oil

2 tbsp red wine vinegar

DINNER

salt

What to do:
1. Ask your grown-up helper to pre-heat the oven to 180°C/Gas Mark 4.
2. Put the chopped tomatoes in a large salad bowl.
3. Tear the bread into chunks.
4. Ask your grown-up helper to put the bread on a baking tray in the oven for about 10 mins.
5. Allow to cool.
6. Add the garlic, peppers and olives to the bowl of tomatoes and give everything a good mix.
7 Tear up the basil leaves with your hands and add to the bowl.
8. Add the olive oil and vinegar and mix everything together.
9. Add the bread and give everything a really good mix.

Burgers

Makes enough for 4

You will need:

400g minced beef or soya mince

1 egg

Dried herbs (e.g. thyme or rosemary)

Salt and pepper

What to do:

1. Ask your grown-up helper to turn on the grill.
2. Mix the mince, dried herbs and egg in a bowl together with a pinch of salt and pepper.
3. When it's all mixed together well, take tablespoonfuls of mixture and shape into balls.
4. Flatten the balls with your hand until they are burger shaped.
5. Ask your grown-up helper to pop the burgers under the grill for 15-20 mins until they are cooked through.

★ TOP TIP ★

Serve your burgers in rolls with lettuce and tomato.

Thin Crust Pizza

Makes 2 large pizzas, serves 4.

You will need:
Base:

300g strong bread flour

200ml warm water

1 tsp instant yeast
(from a sachet or a tub)

1 tsp salt

1 tbsp olive oil

Topping:
Whatever you like! It could be cheese, ham, tuna, onions, peppers, mushrooms.

What to do:
1. Ask your grown-up helper to heat the oven to 240°C/Gas Mark 8
2. Put the flour into a large bowl and stir in the yeast and salt.
3. Make a well, pour in the warm water and the olive oil and bring together with a spoon until you have a soft, fairly wet dough.
4. Turn onto a lightly floured surface and knead for 5 mins until smooth.
5. Roll out the dough into two large circles. They need to be very thin, as they will rise in the oven.
6. Place the dough carefully on to a baking tray.
7. Scatter your choice of toppings over the pizza base.
8. Ask your grown-up helper to place in the oven for 8-10 mins until crisp.

TOP TIP

If you like, you can spread some of your easy tomato sauce on to your pizza with a spoon.

Easy Tomato Pasta Sauce

Makes enough for 2

You will need:

- ✔ 6 large tomatoes
- ✔ Dried herbs (e.g. rosemary, chives, basil)
- ✔ 8 black or green olives (optional)
- ✔ Olive oil, for drizzling
- ✔ Cheddar or parmesan cheese (grated)

TOP TIP

Keep any yummy leftover sauce in the freezer to eat another day.

What to do:

1. Put the tomatoes into a large bowl. Reach down into the bowl and squeeze each one hard until it bursts! Watch out, they'll squirt! Pull the tomatoes to pieces.
2. Add the dried herbs to the tomatoes. Then, if you are using them, tear the olives in half and throw them in too.
3. Add a dribble of olive oil and serve with cooked pasta or any other dish that takes your fancy.
4. Sprinkle some cheese on top.

Stick the bow on Hello Kitty!

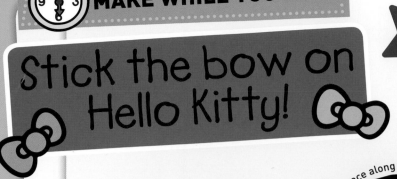

This is a great game to play when you have a sleepover!

DINNER

Trace along the dotted lines.

You will need:

At least one friend

A blindfold

Tracing paper

Pens

White tack

What to do:

1. Trace around the Hello Kitty head and bow, then draw them onto paper and cut them out carefully.
2. Stick Hello Kitty on a wall.
3. Add a small amount of white tack or similar to the back of the bow.
4. Each player takes it in turn to be blindfolded. Spin the blindfolded player around a few times.
5. Have the blindfolded player reach out with the paper bow in hand and try to stick it on Hello Kitty's head.
6. The player who gets the bow closest to where it should be wins!

Trace along the dotted lines.

Ask a grown-up to help you with the tracing.

DINNER

21

Treats!

These mouth-watering treats are so simple to make and even better to eat!

Strawberry Ice Cream

Makes 1 litre

You will need:

400g strawberries

250g mascarpone

200g condensed milk

Cones and sprinkles to serve

What to do:

1. Pull the green hulls out of the strawberries.
2. Tip the strawberries into a flat-bottomed dish.
3. Use a potato masher to squash the strawberries as much as you can. Ask your grown-up helper to give you a hand if you need to.
4. Add the mascarpone and mash this in. Don't worry if it's a bit lumpy. Add the condensed milk and mix everything together. It doesn't matter if the mix is streaky.
5. Spoon the mixture into a metal or plastic box and put in the freezer. Wait until the next day or at least 6 hours before scooping into bowls or cones.

Peanut Butter Cookies

Makes about 24 cookies

You will need:

180g peanut butter

200g brown sugar

1 egg

1 tsp baking powder

What to do:

1. Get your grown-up helper to pre-heat the oven to 180°C/Gas Mark 4.
2. Mix the peanut butter and sugar until it's all combined.
3. Add the egg and baking soda until it's all mixed.
4. Roll the mixture into small balls and place on to a baking tray.
5. Flatten each ball slightly with a fork.
6. Get your grown-up helper to bake them in the oven for 10 mins.
7. Let the cookies cool completely on a wire rack.

TREATS

Create Your Own Ice-Cream Sundae!

What to do:
Simply write your answers under each question and hey presto! A simple recipe for a delicious ice cream sundae. Remember, there are no right or wrong answers – it's whatever you feel like at the time!

Things to decide:

Flavour(s) of ice cream

....

....

....

Sauce (e.g. chocolate sauce, strawberry syrup, jam, honey)

....

....

....

Anything else on top (e.g. chocolate, wafers, nuts, sweets, fruit)

....

....

....

Other decorations (e.g. sparklers, mini umbrellas)

....

....

....

Bowl, glass or cone

....

....

....

Number of spoons

....

....

....

TREATS

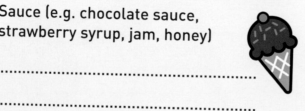

NOW THERE'S ONLY ONE THING LEFT TO DO... GO AND MAKE IT!!

Draw a picture of your yummy ice cream sundae here!

Lemonade

Makes 1 jug

You will need:

3 lemons (chopped)

140g sugar

1 litre water

What to do:

1. Put the chopped up lemons (remove any pips), sugar and half the water in a blender. Ask your grown-up helper to do any chopping.
2. Ask your grown-up helper to blend until the lemon is finely chopped.
3. Pour the mix into a sieve over a bowl and press through as much as you can.
4. Add the rest of the water and more sugar if it's too sour.

10¢

hello kitty lemonade

Yummy!

Banana Bread

Makes 1 loaf

You will need:

120g caster sugar

360g self raising flour

1 egg

200ml milk

50g butter

3 bananas (mashed)

What to do:

1. Get your grown-up helper to pre-heat the oven to 180°C/Gas Mark 4.
2. Grease a loaf tin with butter or margarine.
3. Put the sugar and flour in a bowl.
4. Ask your grown-up helper to melt the butter.
5. Add the melted butter, milk and the egg and mix well.
6. When it's all mixed, add the mashed bananas.
7. Pour into the tin and ask your grown-up helper to bake it for 1 hour, or until it sounds hollow.

Apple Ice

Makes enough for 4

You will need:

500ml water

500ml apple juice

50g icing sugar

What to do:

1. Mix all the ingredients together in a bowl until the sugar is dissolved.
2. Pour the mixture into an airtight container and put in the freezer.
3. After 30 mins stir the mixture.
4. When you want to eat it, stir the frozen mixture with a fork so it breaks up a bit.

Honey Buns

Makes 12

You will need:

115g self raising flour

115g butter

2 eggs

115g honey

55g chocolate chips or chunks

What to do:

1. Get your grown-up helper to pre-heat the oven to 180°C/Gas Mark 4.
2. Beat the honey and butter together.
3. Add eggs, flour and chocolate and mix well.
4. Spoon into muffin cases.
5. Ask your grown-up helper to pop the muffins into the oven for 15-20 mins until golden.

Meringues

Makes enough for 4

You will need:

4 egg whites

220g sugar

What to do:

1. Get your grown-up helper to pre-heat the oven to 140°C/Gas Mark 1.
2. Divide the egg whites from the yolks.
3. Put your egg whites in a very clean bowl.
4. Whisk!
5. Once the egg whites are stiff and don't wobble, add the sugar a bit at a time and keep whisking.
6. Stop once the mixture is thick and glossy.
7. Line a baking sheet with greaseproof paper.
8. Spoon heaped tablespoons of the mixture onto the greaseproof paper.
9. Ask your grown-up helper to cook them for 45-60 mins until they are crisp on the outside.
10. Ask your grown-up helper to leave them to cool in the oven with the door slightly open.

Fruit Mess

Makes enough for 4

You will need:

4 x meringues

Tub of cream (or thick yoghurt)

As much fruit as you like.

What to do:

1. If you're using cream, whip until it thickens.
2. Stir most of your fruit into the cream or yoghurt.
3. Break up your meringues and carefully stir them into the cream or yoghurt. Leave a little bit of meringue to sprinkle on top.
4. Place the cream or yoghurt mix in a bowl and sprinkle over the rest of the fruit and the meringue.

★ TOP TIP ★

Using different fruits completely changes the flavour!

29

Coconut Cakes

Makes 24 cakes

You will need:
2 eggs

100g caster sugar

160g desiccated coconut

What to do:

1. Ask your grown-up helper to heat the oven to 180°C/Gas mark 4.
2. Lightly grease a baking tray.
3. Separate the eggs and put the yolks to one side.
4. Mix the egg whites, sugar and coconut in a bowl with a spoon until well-combined and then pour the mixture on to a clean worktop.
5. Shape into a rectangle and press down with your hands to flatten until it's about 1cm thick.
6. Use a small biscuit cutter or a cup to cut out rounds and place them on a baking tray.
7. Ask your grown-up helper to bake in the oven for 12-15 mins, until golden. Cool on a wire rack.

Sponge Cake

TOP TIP

This sponge cake tastes delicious served with ice cream!

You will need:
225g butter or margarine

225g caster sugar

4 medium eggs

225g self raising flour

Jam

What to do:

1. Get your grown-up helper to preheat the oven to 180°C/Gas Mark 4.
2. Beat the butter and sugar together until it's pale.
3. Beat in the eggs.
4. Add the flour.
5. Place the mix in two greased tins and ask your grown-up helper to bake for 20-25 mins.
6. Let cool, then sandwich the cakes with jam.

TREATS

Hello Kitty Stencil

This is a bit fiddly so you may want to ask your grown-up helper to cut out your Hello Kitty stencil.

Cut along the dotted lines.

If you don't want to cut up your book, trace this stencil.

How to use your lovely Hello Kitty stencil.
Once you've made your lovely cake, then use this gorgeous Hello Kitty stencil to make it really extra special. Simply place on the cool cake then sprinkle away with icing sugar.

31

TOP ★ TIP ★

For a sweet treat use chocolate powder instead of icing sugar.

Yummy! Yummy! In your tummy!

Cut along the dotted lines.

TREATS

32